I'm Off To See The Wizard

Johnny Hart and Brant Parker

CORONET BOOKS
Hodder Fawcett, London

Copyright © 1971, 1972 by Field Newspaper Syndicate

Copyright © 1976 by Fawcett Publications Inc.,
New York

First published 1976 by Fawcett Publications, Inc.

Coronet edition 1978

Printed and bound in Great Britain for
Hodder and Stoughton Paperbacks, a
division of Hodder and Stoughton Ltd.,
Mill Road, Dunton Green, Sevenoaks,
Kent (Editorial Office: 47 Bedford
Square, London, WC1 3DP) by
Hunt Barnard Printing Ltd.,
Aylesbury, Bucks.

ISBN 0 340 22297 2

10-5

10-7

10-8

10-12

11-4

11-8

11·12

CRANK
CRANK
CRANK
CRANK
CRANK
CRANK
CRANK
CRANK
CRANK
CRANK
CRANK

3

12-4

12-18

4

12-29

1-7

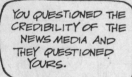

5

1-27

A WITCH HAS CAST A SPELL ON MY WIFE... SHE WILL SLEEP UNTIL KISSED BY A HANDSOME PRINCE.

2-2

I WILL SEND OUT FOR A PRINCE IMMEDIATELY.

MAKE SURE YOU FIND ONE THAT DRINKS.

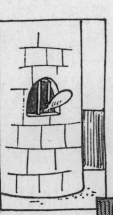

I THINK I'LL ENROLL IN A NIGHT COURSE.

2-7

...IT'S IMPORTANT FOR A WIFE TO CONTINUE HER EDUCATION.

BLAB

PLEASE LET IT BE SOMETHING TO DO WITH COOKING!

32

3.3

3·B

GREAT NEWS, SIRE!

...RODNEY WAS NAMED "MOST VALUABLE PLAYER" AT TODAY'S GAMES!

HOW SO?

HE WORE HIS DIAMOND SCABBARD.

WHAT'S IT LIKE OUTSIDE?

3-28

BLURRY.

4-3

4.5

4-8

4-10

LAST ONE IN, IS A ROTTEN EGG!

4-15

4-24

FOR YOUR **25 YEARS** OF **FAITHFUL SERVICE,** I PRESENT YOU WITH THIS CERTIFICATE, SIGNED BY THE **KING.**

5-1

THANK YOU! I'LL HAVE THIS FRAMED AND HANG IT, FOR **ALL** OF MY FAMILY TO SEE!

WHO HUNG THE CITATION OVER THE HALF MOON?

5-3

5-9

8

MARTHA, WE CAN'T AFFORD TO GO OUT THIS SATURDAY NIGHT.

5-11

SO?

SO, WHEN I WAKE UP SUNDAY MORNING, HIT ME ON THE HEAD WITH THIS HAMMER.

5·12

S-23

5-25

S-27

MORE MAGIC FROM THE WIZARD OF ID

JOHNNY HART and BRANT PARKER

All these books are available at your local bookshop or newsagent, or can be ordered direct from the publisher. Just tick the titles you want and fill in the form below.

Prices and availability subject to change without notice.

CORONET BOOKS, P.O. Box 11, Falmouth, Cornwall.

Please send cheque or postal order, and allow the following for postage and packing:

U.K. – One book 22p plus 10p per copy for each additional book ordered, up to a maximum of 32p.

B.F.P.O. and EIRE – 22p for the first book plus 10p per copy for the next 6 books, thereafter 4p per book.

OTHER OVERSEAS CUSTOMERS – 30p for the first book and 10p per copy for each additional book.

Name ....

Address ....

....